PIXIE DUST V

A TALE OF COMBATTING CORPORATE BURNOUT: PROTECTING YOUR TALENT

http://www.fast-print.net/bookshop

PIXIE DUST V:
A TALE OF COMBATTING CORPORATE BURNOUT:
PROTECTING YOUR TALENT
Copyright © Howard G Awbery 2015

A catalogue record for this book is available from the British Library

ISBN 978-178456-229-8

First published 2015 by
FASTPRINT PUBLISHING
Peterborough, England.

Foreword

For a start, we need to stop calling everyday stress burnout. Burnout is not just stress. Burnout is complex and culminates in a complete inability to get out of bed, tie shoelaces or choose what clothes to wear; an incapability to undertake work of any capacity; an addictive, overwhelming exhaustion; a condition resulting in disillusionment and a dysfunctional attitude towards work, colleagues and family.

All levels of leadership experience workplace stress from time to time, but to describe leaders going through a busy time or temporary rough patch as 'burnt out' denigrates the seriousness of the real condition and mitigates the culpability of the organisations which have stood by and watched it happen to our talented leaders.

With talent at a premium, there are a number of steps organisations can take to reduce the possibility of their leaders burning out. For a start, is 24/7 communication really necessary? Is working on a hands-free phone whilst driving acceptable when the indisputable research says the driver's reaction time is worse than if over the UK alcohol limit? Is breakfast with an iPhone, lunch on the run and dinner with a laptop how we want our leaders to function?

Why not consider flexible, annual work patterns based on operational demands, lateral development to combat repetitive work

2

and routine mentor meetings to identify early signs of burnout? Promoting healthy eating and exercise can also be highly effective. Some organisations are already seeing a difference by discounting gym membership, providing fresh fruit, insisting on regular breaks and stamping out the sandwich at the keyboard culture.

While all these are positive steps, nothing can replace the need for realism. The most significant thing that organisations can do is to look at the workloads of leaders and ask, honestly, is this a realistic expectation?

www.awberymanagement.co.uk/pixie-dust

Illustrations by Colleen Capewell

Cover by James Bucklow

The Ten-Tree-Wood Story so far…

PIXIE DUST: A Tale of Recruitment Problems in Ten-Tree-Wood.

A well-deserved promotion creates a vacancy in Ten-Tree-Wood's Senior Management Team. To fill the vacancy and find his perfect 'Number 2', Floot, the Community Leader, undertakes the selection process for a new Number 2 in the conventional, outmoded way. Finally, he chooses the pretty one and ends up with the, not unfamiliar, 'appointment from hell.'

Discussions with Floot's previous 'Number 2', Harebell, with whom he had formed a 'high performing management dyad', culminated in the two of them documenting a scientific process of closer matching senior managers with potential 'number 2s'. Every senior manager should seriously consider applying this process! Next time around using this scientific process, Floot chose a new Number 2 with whom he quickly formed a high performing management dyad.

PIXIE DUST II: Leading Change

When change was necessary in Ten-Tree-Wood it was all too easy for Community Leader Floot to drop unintentionally into the management style of imposition. The resulting disconnect between the drivers of change and the recipients of change led to an inevitable disaster. Following the imposition of change, Floot's Senior Management Team considered the alternative i.e. engaging the assistance of the 'stars' within the invisible culture of the community. Once communicated with correctly, the 'stars' engaged the support of all the folk within their 'influential spheres' and the required change proceeded at a pace that staggered the Senior Management Team.

PIXIE DUST III: Effective Management Networking

eaders have too little time to spend at the wrong networking events or doing the wrong things at the right networking events. Floot, the Community Leader of Ten-Tree-Wood, is sent on a learning journey to discover why some communities flourish by using networking. On his journey he discovered that attending a networking event solely as a 'taker' can have painful consequences. He discovered the secret to the process was **FOSHOD.** i.e. **F**ocus, **O**ffer of Skills, **S**entence of Introduction, **H**elpful Introductions, **O**utstandingly Smart and **D**o your Homework- **FOSHOD**.

Floot also discovered there is an apprenticeship to complete prior to becoming a member of any really valuable management network.

PIXIE DUST IV: A Tale of Transforming Low Performing Managers into High Performing Leaders

Acrisis in Ten-Tree-Wood demonstrates to Floot that he is the problem. His management style of micro-managing as a means of improving performance is as naively misguided as it is widely held. He seeks to modify his style by talking with his number 2 and hears about In and Out Managers, The Pygmalion Effect and the Golem effect. Following six months of coaching by Floot, a further crisis demonstrates he has significantly influenced the performance of two of his Senior Team and transformed them from poor performing managers into high performing leaders.

Dedication

Many thanks to all those who influenced my thinking… Professor Max Blythe, Schaufeli and Enzan, Freudenberger, Michael Bader, Tim Casserley and Professor David Megginson's book, 'Learning from Burnout'. Mary Sisson, Professor Sing Manaux, Zeus and Skiffington, Jane Rawden, Tim Awbery, Melin Homes, AXA PPP Health, Asset Skills, Professor Christina Maslach, Rob David, Dr Arun Midha, Phyllis Northcott, Dr Andy Bibby, Yoda, Dr Geoff Mackey, Bob Buckley, Ollie Scheyer, Dr Joe Dearden, Karen Morris, Tracey Pepper, Richard Branson, Wendy Hambleton, John Osborne, Colleen Capewell, James Bucklow, Ben Quain, Penny Williams, Sarah Davis, Eluned Handcock and John Holliday.

And all those leaders who were prepared to share their personal burnout recovery stories with me.

Contents

Chapter One

THE TEN-TREE-WOOD LIBRARY

Lord Seren coughed as he blew the dust from a weighty, leather bound book extricated from a high shelf in the library. The motes of dust shone in the sunlight as they floated down in the lonely silence. Some of these antique books had not seen the light of day for years but Lord Seren knew they contained 'ancient wisdom'. In these books he knew he would find the answer to the Central Domain's, short-sighted, headlong race to deplete a rapidly diminishing talent pool by burning out its leaders.

Lord Seren held the very senior position of Critical Friend and Sage to the Central Domain Queen who reigned over twelve woodland communities. His role was to advise, guide and offer notes of caution and encouragement. During his term in office he had seen many queens come and go but the current queen was by far the most demanding.

The old sage's mind was in a troubled state for as the new queen's time in office lengthened, the pace of the woodland commercial world was accelerating. In its wake he observed a significant number of the Central Domain's top talent completely burnout. To find a solution to this terrible waste, Lord Seren had set himself the task of trying to understand what was actually happening. To achieve this he was analysing the Central Domain's corporate culture, trying to understand what were the catalysts that created burnout and trying to establish how best he could support those leaders who were past helping themselves.

Of the highflying leaders who had already completely burnt out, a small number had terminated their careers because they were unable to undertake work in any capacity. These leaders were in a very serious state and needed long recovery periods. Lord Seren observed that they suffered from an addictive, overwhelming, relentless exhaustion, a condition resulting in disillusionment and often a dysfunctional attitude towards work, colleagues and family.

Workplace stress is a common enough phenomenon experienced by leaders at all levels of their careers from time to time, but Lord Seren noticed it had started to become fashionable by some of the more histrionic leaders to describe their behaviour during a temporary busy period as being 'burnt out'.

The more he understood about burnout the more incensed he became by this designer description. Their problem was not burnout! What they were describing was a bit of tiredness, a temporary increase in the demands on their time. This grossly exaggerated description of their tiredness denigrated the seriousness of the real condition, trivialised those incapacitated by true burnout but, most importantly, it mitigated the culpability of the Central Domain Queen who created the culture and, worst of all, watched it happen.

On the other hand, there were some leaders in this new, fast paced culture who were thriving on the pressures, which intrigued him.

However, his interest was in those not coping particularly well and sadly he could identify a few who were spiralling downward towards complete burnout. In particular, Lord Seren was watching a community leader named Floot, the leader of one of the Central Domain's toughest communities called Ten-Tree-Wood.

Until two years ago, Ten-Tree-Wood had been a disaster of a community. It had been described by the Central Domain as 'a festering sore' and was seen financially as an, 'arterial bleeder'.

There had been little leadership exercised by the previous senior leadership team and in-fighting was commonplace. Ten-Tree-Wood's debts to the Central Domain had been soaring and there had been little to endear the community to anyone. That is, until Floot arrived on the scene. Floot took the community in hand, cleared out the ineffective leaders, recruited a solid, senior leadership team and transformed the community. Much to the surprise of the Central Domain, the community debts had all but been repaid and now it had become one of the most sought after communities in which to live. He had taken complete control of the Ten-Tree-Wood community and the previous Domain Queen had described Floot as a 'totemic leader'.

However, nothing stays the same for long in woodland life and when the much-loved Domain Queen retired a new queen was appointed. This was a queen who had aspirations for an early promotion to the Supreme Court and as such, treasured her own vision without any acknowledgement of her new Domain's recent past. She set new, tougher targets for all of her twelve communities.

Despite its recent turbulent history, Ten-Tree-Wood did not escape these tougher targets. Higher targets meant the competition for trade between the woodland communities would be much fiercer, the margins on every deal would be smaller, the volumes of work for the same return would be greater, the taxes higher, the workdays longer and technology was driving everything. The new Domain Queen's ambition was to establish her reputation by double-digit growth from her twelve communities.

Sadly, Lord Seren had been watching community leader after community leader straining under the burden of the work culture of the new Domain Queen. These were not lazy leaders out for an easy ride, for the previous Domain Queen had chosen these leaders with great care and the one thing they all had in common was the descriptor of being a 'high-performer'. However, under the new Domain Queen every leader was working harder than they had ever worked before and some were frightened of losing their jobs.

Early into her new regime a number of leaders started to lose self-esteem and as a consequence became significantly less productive. To hide this diminishing performance they compensated by working longer hours and the insidious downhill journey had begun. Some leaders were working every evening and every weekend and, as a result, were grinding themselves down towards complete burnout.

Often the objective of these leaders was to try to protect their teams from criticism or redundancy.

What Lord Seren found strange was that some leaders were able to cope with the new stress and some even thrived. He visualised these successful leaders as though they were walking quickly at the top of a downward moving escalator. When the speed or workload fluctuated these leaders coped with the changes of pace and stayed firmly at the top.

Lord Seren described these leaders as Resilient Leaders.

Resilient Leaders

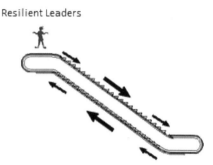

Lord Seren also observed that some leaders who found it more difficult to cope with the increased pace, were gradually carried down the escalator no matter how hard they worked. These leaders were suffering from the early signs of burning out. However, anywhere between the top and a third of the way down the virtual escalator they were able to step off unaided and reflect on what was happening to them.

Independently, they came to the conclusion that focussing on increased hours alone was an unsustainable solution. Their reflections led them to consider what else could they change, e.g. more development of individuals in their teams, followed by more delegation, more effective prioritising, having difficult performance conversations with some members of their team and having frank conversations with their line leaders. After a little time to recover and implement the changes, these leaders were able to return to the top of the escalator.

Lord Seren described these leaders as 'Self Recoverers'.

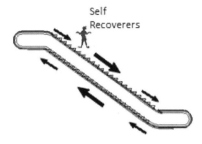

Then there were the myopic leaders who couldn't see what was happening to them and were carried two thirds of the way down the escalator. By two thirds of the way down they needed a 'Recovery Buddy' to help them step off. Once off the escalator the task of the 'Recovery Buddy' was to coach the leader back up to the top by helping them develop a personal recovery strategy. A personal recovery strategy tailored to address the exact circumstances that were causing the leader to burn out.

Both of these leaders were burning out but definitely not burnt out. Their position was one from which it was eminently recoverable. Nevertheless, if there were no positive changes in their behaviour they would eventually find themselves at the bottom of the escalator, completely burnt out.

Lord Seren described these leaders as 'Assisted Recoverers'.

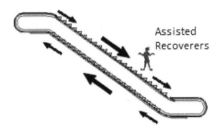

Finally, there were those leaders who completely burnt out and burnt out meant exactly that; they were unable to function, not capable of getting out of bed, tie a shoe lace or choose clothes for the day.

Of these leaders Lord Seren discovered that there were three types who hit the bottom of the escalator, all of whom had been high-flyers in their day.

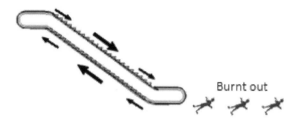

Burnt out

A small group of these completely burnt out leaders recovered by completely changing their life aspirations. They abandoned their current employer and sought a less stressful job e.g. stacking shelves in the woodland store. Lord Seren considered this to be a complete waste of leadership talent and huge denigration of the Domain Queen who claimed to be 'a caring employer of choice'. Stories create reputation and, as with a poor restaurant meal, seventeen times as many folk hear about a bad employer experience as those who hear about a good employer experience.

The second group of completely burnt out leaders, by far the majority, never returned to their previous level of responsibility but had their careers 'frozen' in less senior positions. Here nobody won, observed Lord Seren, for the accommodated casualty now wore the 'invisible life-long badge' of having 'completely burnt out'. Many accepted the position with lower levels of responsibility but suffered some loss of self-esteem. Here, through the lack of early intervention, the Domain lost yet another high-flyer, but being a 'caring employer' the casualty often retained their original salary despite not carrying the commensurate level of responsibility or accountability. Retained their salary that is, until a new senior leader with no emotional attachment to the casualty's history made the justifiable financial decision and sacked them!

***

Finally, a very small group of leaders learned priceless lessons from their journey to the bottom of the escalator experience. This very small group eventually recovered fully and re-asserted their position in the corporate hierarchy. Shortly afterwards, exceeding their previous levels of responsibility and accountability.

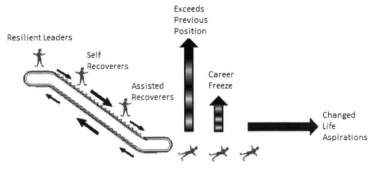

The quest for an explanation why some leaders burnt out and others did not was worrying Lord Seren; for if he had a better understanding, then he may be able to help the less fortunate leaders by early recognition of their situation. By having a better understanding he hoped to be able to recommend a better culture, eradicate some of the catalysts that created burnout and help those who found it difficult to create a recovery strategy on their own. Anything was better than just watching the Central Domain's talent, at all levels, crashing and burning around him.

Whenever he was faced with a situation that made his brain hurt, Lord Seren went back to first principles. What happened in the animal kingdom? There was generally a parallel. This approach had served him well in the past and he saw no reason why the ancient wisdom contained inside the books, wouldn't lead to answers now.

Just like the community leaders who were working at maximum capacity, Lord Seren was trying to understand how animals could run at astonishing speed when being chased by predators. The research from the ancient books had so far led him to believe that animals could exert extraordinary bursts of energy, but only for short periods of time and this depended on their health and maturity.

'So, physical health and experience were vitally important,' concluded Lord Seren.

Some animals were able to display basic emotions like surprise and fear, which would be communicated to other animals. 'So, it would be reasonable to assume,' conjectured Lord Seren, that...

'Community leaders, when under stress would display and communicate complex emotions.'

However, some animals, in particular those that regularly had to fight for survival, created periods of stress-free recovery time without which, their physical output under stress degraded.

'**So, sleep and recovery periods were vitally important,**' concluded Lord Seren to himself.

Without this stress-free time the day came when they were unable to run anymore and lay down accepting their fate, completely burnt out!

If this was 'ancient wisdom' in animal biology then why, after prolonged periods of excessive stress, did it come as such a surprise to folk when a high-performing woodland leader lay down, completely burnt out.

"Who'd have thought it?" mimicked Lord Seren to himself.

Lord Seren turned his attention to Floot, the highly respected woodland leader of Ten-Tree-Wood. He had watched Floot's output of work slow down to a pedestrian pace compared with his previous outstanding performance. Currently, Floot had lost his spark, looked grey, his temper was quicker to surface, he was making mistakes, the quality of what he was doing had deteriorated and Ten-Tree-Wood's reputation was becoming tarnished by him not delivering on promises.

Floot was burning out and it was becoming infectious. Those around him were finding him harder to work with which, in turn, was stressing them out trying to keep up. Floot's behaviour was breeding behaviour. Everyone else, but Floot, could see it.

He decided he would intervene before Floot added his name to the sad graveyard of burnt out leaders.

Lord Seren shook his head in despair, for he knew nobody would take ownership to assist Floot but they would all stand by and watch him tearing himself apart trying to cope... and they would do precisely nothing because they had no idea what to do!

Or so he thought for that wasn't entirely fair or true. At that precise moment, the remaining three senior leaders of Ten-Tree-Wood called Dai-Full-Pelt, the community's number 2, Dandelion the HR Manager and Barley their Critical Friend, were getting together secretly to decide what to do about their leader Floot and what the impact of him burning out was having on the Ten-Tree-Wood community.

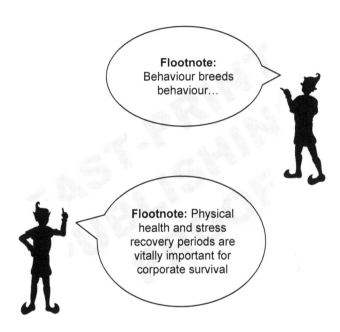

Chapter Two

A SECRET MEETING

Dai-Full-Pelt opened the secret meeting: "Thank you Dandelion and Barley for coming."

He was speaking at the hurriedly convened, secret meeting of three of Ten-Tree-Wood's Senior Leadership Team. The team members present consisted of Dandelion, the very traditional HR Manager who had a reputation for going into an industrial relations situation that was just simmering and quickly bringing it to the boil. Dai-Full-Pelt, the quiet dormouse and number 2 of the hugely successful Ten-Tree-Wood community, jokingly named for his slow, deep deliberation and finally, Barley the badger, their thoughtful, Critical Friend. The three were discussing the inconsistent behaviour of their well-respected, high-performing leader Floot, who gave the appearance of burning out.

Floot, the leader of Ten-Tree-Wood's community, normally thrived under pressure, but was currently struggling with the volume of changes and enhanced targets he was now expected to achieve. The newly appointed Domain Queen had been sweeping through putting her stamp firmly on each of her twelve communities. Established procedures were being challenged, age-old customs and practices were being thrown out and new age thinking and technology was being imposed at pace.

Floot completely accepted that things could not stand still and in the name of progress much would have to change. But it was the pace and volume of change that was such a burden. It wasn't the complexity or challenge of any one project that was grinding him down. On the contrary, he revelled in big new challenges; it was the incessant volume of change that made him feel he wasn't achieving anything. As a true professional, Floot had been loyal to the new Domain Queen, but even his loyalty had been stretched to a fine thread. Now he found it hard to be positive about anything she said. Currently, Floot was off chasing his tail for information demanded of him before close of play that very day.

Dai-Full-Pelt held the floor of the secret meeting. The three of them had given examples of Floot's behaviour and there was a consensus that the situation had now become very serious. Dai-Full-Pelt who, as usual, had done his research, was now trying to explain medically what was happening to Floot.

"Floot's diminishing ability to cope is due to the prolonged over-use of his body's coping processes, triggered by the pressure he's been under. In response to such stressors, all higher animals resort to a complex set of internal emergency changes that reinforce their coping potential, called the stress response."

"I'll explain what this means. Stress, switches on sub-conscious nervous system responses sending nerve impulses around the body that increase the heart rate and blood circulation. Similarly, these nerve impulses prompt various glands to release hormones like a dandelion losing its seeds in a high wind."

"These hormones mobilise glucose supplies from storage tissue increasing available energy to run, to work or to fight. At the same time, hormones that are not required for the current pressures like tissue maintenance, reproduction and the immune system are all shut down."

"This stress response has evolved over many years to improve our performance in stressful, short-term circumstances when our performance can be amazing. But problems arise when we call on our stress response hormones too often over long periods of time, just as Floot is doing now. His stress response has steadily turned from friend to foe."

Dandelion yawned loudly and through the yawn declared: "I don't know anything about all that stuff but Floot's trying to do a million things, he's forgetting loads, he's forever got a cold or flu and is as snappy as a ferret with toothache! I suggested he talk to Occupational Health people from the Central Domain and have two weeks off and he snapped, 'I don't have time for all that nonsense!'"

"Exactly!" said Dai-Full-Pelt. "Things that would normally take him minutes to complete are now taking him forever, he's making mistake after mistake and due to his anxiety he's finding it hard to sleep properly. Because he's losing sleep, a downward spiral of performance has gathered momentum and he's too close to see it. And that my friends, is exactly what we are watching unfold in front of us. Floot's downward spiral of performance is commonly known as 'burning out'."

"So what are we going to do?" enquired Dandelion, who wasn't the most patient HR Manager but had held a candle for Floot for many years and didn't like what she was watching."

"We can't do anything," said Dai-Full-Pelt., "He has to do it himself. He has to realise where he is on this personal journey and it is he who has to stop and take measures to reverse the trend in his behaviour."

Dai-Full-Pelt pushed his glasses onto the top of his head and, shaking his head, sighed for his friend.

Barley intervened: "I'm not at all sure he recognises that his performance is as bad as we believe it is, but just as Dai-Full-Pelt says, he needs to acknowledge he has a problem before he can address it."

The three pondered this point in silence.

"But can't we just take some of the load off him?" asked Dandelion.

"Yes we could, but what will happen if we do? He'll just fill the space with taking longer to do the things he's currently undertaking, another thing will come to the top of his priority list and he'll become even more anxious about something else."

"We'll do him no favours in the long run by taking work away from him. It will make him feel less valued, he'll start to feel guilty that he can't cope and it will be another tangible example that he's letting us all down. By taking things off him we'll significantly and adversely affect his mental attitude and self-worth which, in turn, will affect his capability."

"Well, we can't just watch him grind himself into the ground," remonstrated Dandelion, with her hands held out in supplication.
She continued: "Do you think it's a fear that he will be seen to fail as community leader or is it guilt that he will let us, his Senior Leadership Team, down?"

Then Dandelion said the unthinkable: "Could it be that he has actually peaked and we have to accept that he just can't keep up his previous pace anymore? Maybe, he needs to accept a smaller community and freeze his career?"

Another long silence ensued as they digested the unthinkable.

It was the thoughtful Barley who suggested a solution: "What do we do in Ten-Tree-Wood when we don't know what to do?"

"What do you mean, what do we do when we don't know what to do? You're not making any sense Barley!" snapped the irritated Dandelion, in her all too familiar HR growl.

"If we have a leak we fetch a plumber to mend it. If we have a broken window we fetch a glazier in to fix it. What I mean is, we fetch someone in who has fixed the problem before or has experienced the same symptoms and found a solution."

"So, what you're suggesting," clarified Dai-Full-Pelt very slowly and thoughtfully, "is we seek advice from someone who has been on the same downward spiral of performance that Floot is on now, but who has found a way to recover."

"Exactly."

"Who?"

"I don't know yet, but I'm sure there are folk."

"I know," chipped in Dandelion, "Bap-bap. Bap-bap the baker became very disorganised in his behaviour and started suffering delusions. He ended up withdrawing from Ten-Tree-Wood society completely."

"No," corrected Dai-Full-Pelt, "Bap-bap was suffering from an extreme form of mental illness. Mental illness is a completely different thing from work place burnout. Floot doesn't have a mental illness although in some extreme cases burnout can result in a form of depression. Floot's suffering from a working environment that, if by some magic, reverted back to how it used to be, he would quickly return to being able to cope."

If the working environment is unlikely to revert back to how it was, then Floot has to develop a coping strategy of his own. With mental illness like Bap-bap, it doesn't matter what changes were made to his working environment, nothing would have had any impact on him whatsoever without psychotherapy and or medication."

The three fell silent again. After a long pause it was Dai-Full-Pelt who spoke.

"I believe I can think of three local folk who have displayed symptoms of burning out."

"Who?"

"Well, one person is Old Snoz, the apothecary. Old Snoz was a lovely, caring man who went out of his way to help folk and was loved by all the children in the community. However, in his case he became so cynical and negative through overload of work, he started to believe the people he was trying to help, deserved their misfortune through over-eating, over-drinking and lack of exercise and in no uncertain terms told them so! He was burning out and suffered a complete change to his personality."

"Floot's gone like that, all negative and cynical," reflected Dandelion. "Only the other day I suggested he employ a PA and he snapped back saying, 'He'd spend all day telling them what to do then end up having to do it himself to get it right. He might as well do it himself in the first place'. It's not like him at all."

"Then there's Tink the dealer. Tink is a loveable rogue, who quietly does lots of good things for less well-off folk in the community, but because he was always chasing sales and ridiculous self-imposed targets he never felt he was achieving anything. He actually was but he never felt that he was."

"Yes," said Barley. "Floot's just the same, rushing about trying to do everything like a butterfly, leaving it all half-finished and having to go back to complete things later in the evening or at weekends."

Dai-Full-Pelt nodded confirming this thought and continued: "The third person is Dai-Bones the funeral director. Dai-Bones went to pieces during the long, bad winter months with all the trade he had to deal with. As the bitter winter went on and on he just couldn't keep up and became so tired he ended up making coffins of all the wrong sizes for folk. He squashed enormous folk into coffins only big enough for fairies so he needed to make extensions at the feet end and he put tiny folk in huge coffins he'd made for Trolls, you could hear them rolling about inside. He just kept saying: 'Oh. It'll do.' It wasn't funny. He became drained of all his emotions."

The three sat quietly recognising the seriousness of Floot's situation unfolding in front of them.

"Floot has advanced stages of all these symptoms," remarked Barley in a quiet voice, "so he's triple burning out".

"But the good news," said Dai-Full-Pelt looking for a spark of anything positive in all the gloom, "is that Old Snoz, Tink and Dai-Bones are all back to their old selves again doing their old jobs or something similar, in fact, they all seem to be coping better than they ever used to. They must all have developed coping strategies that worked for them, so let's get them here secretly to Ten-Tree-Wood HQ to talk to us about what happened to them."

"Let's also invite Lord Seren the Sage,' said Barley. "He met me earlier and said that he had been observing Floot's behaviour and was very concerned. He offered his help and would be pleased to be involved."

"Let's hope that between us all we can find a solution," said Dandelion resignedly, "it's too serious to leave it any longer."

With that they closed their secret meeting and went their separate ways.

FLOOTNOTE: A slow, deterioration in performance may be the early signs of a leader BURNING OUT

Chapter Three - Part One

THREE LEADERS BURNING OUT

(SNOZ THE APOTHECARY)

Snoz was invited to come the next night to talk in secret to Dai-Full-Pelt, Dandelion, Barley and Lord Seren. The four of them sat avidly waiting for his tale.

Snoz sat in front of them in his dark, traditional, apothecary tunic with the pointed hood folded back to reveal a head of thick silver hair. He made himself comfortable ready to tell his tale.

Snoz explained he'd served the Ten-Tree-Wood Community for years, as had his father before him and regularly been invited by other community apothecaries to assist with difficult cases. In the main, he felt everyone, both young and old, held him and his knowledge in high regard. He had studied hard and revelled in the belief that he was one of the best apothecaries in all the woodland communities. There had been peaks and troughs of volume in his work and at times it was stressful but not relentless and he had taken it in his stride. Life had been good; he'd employed three apprentices, felt on top of things and at that time had been buzzing with new ideas.

Prior to the 'bad times' there had been little change to his workload as he had systematically been preaching preventative medicine to his community for years, the result being there was less and less serious illness: a real community success story.

But he explained that what happened next distinctly changed his attitude to life.

Snoz hesitated for a few seconds and then said: "I'm going to find it extremely uncomfortable to explain what happened to me. It was a very difficult time and I'm dredging up some very sensitive issues here that I believed I'd buried for good. If I hesitate whilst looking for the right words please forgive me. I'm not proud of what happened to me."

After a pause he continued with his story: "Some while age now, a new Domain Apothecary was appointed over all the twelve community apothecaries in the Domain and like many new leaders he was a new broom. He instigated many changes that were 'performance-based' rather than 'customer-based'. For someone like me, who had dedicated my whole life to providing a service from my heart, to suddenly have to don a business head, restrict my time per patient to six minutes and charge everyone the same amount regardless of the wealth of the family, presented me with a series of social and moral dilemmas that went against everything for which I stood."

There was not a sound in the room.

Snoz continued, explaining to his audience how he started to become cynical and unsupportive of edicts from above, openly criticising the new Domain Apothecary. Initially, his criticisms were directed at the new Domain Apothecary, but bit-by-bit anger and frustration invaded his whole life and his criticism became targeted at some of his patients.

He went on to explain that previously, he had treated people's ills sympathetically and in a non-judgemental manner, but slowly and surely he started to openly criticise their lifestyles as contributors to their health misfortunes. As a form of stress release from the new culture he started becoming sarcastic towards some of his patients, for instance, he mimicked smokers with their hacking coughs, and he told folk that their hip pains and knee tenderness could be eliminated forever by not trying to eat all the pies and mountains of chips in Ten-Tree-Wood every day. Embarrassed, he recounted that, completely out of character, he had even suggested a sharp slap for a petulant youngster who wouldn't sleep, would be a far better cure than all the potions in the world.

He confessed to the three members of the Senior Leadership Team and Lord Seren that, as a result of the stress, he lost his focus on caring. It became replaced by an angry offloading of stress targeted initially at the Domain Apothecary but gradually affected his judgement when dealing with really sick folk.

He began to hear whispers that folk were beginning to prefer to trek to other communities rather than put up with his rudeness. Worst of all on hearing this, he didn't care. His drop in patient numbers was blamed on the Domain Apothecary and all the nonsense impositions and mountains of paperwork.

Snoz shared with them that he found himself in a place where he didn't know who he was any more and, the really terrible part was, that there were times when it really didn't bother him. He recounted an example to help them understand the depth of the issue at its worst point.

Snoz told them that one day the father of a small child, who had croup, asked Snoz to visit his little girl and give her some medicine. Snoz told the father, 'he was very busy and would come in the morning'. He knew the family of the little girl would have a terrible night with all the coughing. In the morning he found out from one of his apprentices that the father had walked seven miles to the next community to get the necessary medicines and walked the seven miles home rather than have his little girl suffer and be distressed. Snoz shared with them that all he had done when he heard the story was shrug his shoulders. It made him cringe inside just thinking about it now.

The coup de grâce came in the form of a 'Productivity Improvement Initiative' from the Domain Apothecary. To reduce costs, Snoz was told he had to take on half of the patients from the next community. Snoz said he had exploded at the decision. Looking behind the decision he wondered if the Domain Apothecary was increasing the stressors on him to break him, or protect himself from Snoz as a competitor for his position in the future. Snoz had already noted that the Domain Apothecary never gave him credit for anything, further advancing his, 'insecurity of the Domain Apothecary' theory.

Snoz explained it wasn't the challenges that made him listless and not care; it was the volume, same old, same old. He was slowly but surely being sucked into working longer, seeing more people and getting less and less out of his job. On top of that, he had to deal with sick people he didn't know, and deal with them quicker. Overnight he become accountable for taking money off folk who couldn't afford to pay coupled with the mountains of paperwork. It all meant he ended up having to work at weekends. Consequently, there was no recovery time from work and the stress built up and up.

Now there were more folk coughing all over him, more folk sneezing all over him, more folk with warts, more night visits and an even greater number of folk with rashes in places he didn't care to look any more. The situation was going on and on and through his exhaustion he couldn't see what a poor service he was giving. Snoz shared with them that, on looking back, he had become grumpier and grumpier and hated getting out of bed in the mornings. Two of his apprentices had left saying they couldn't stand working with him anymore.

Snoz paused to allow his captive audience time to digest his tale.

Then slowly looking up at the ceiling with a tear in his eye he said: "On reflection, do you know what the worst thing was? The worst thing was I didn't stop. I didn't look at the situation and learn anything when it all started to go wrong. Had I learned from the situation in the first few months I would have been able to sort myself out, behave differently and re-establish control each time the pressure increased. But I got caught up in it. It was like a drug. The Domain Apothecary demanded more and more from me and I just kept delivering to a reasonable standard, as I thought. To cope I just kept doing more and more hours until one day I dropped."

He shared with the spellbound group that what he was doing seemed completely pointless. He even considered changing to a less stressful occupation, like working in a local shop, anything. He found he had stopped believing in what he did. But what was the strangest thing of all was that he started searching for a point to life in general. As if he didn't have enough to worry about in the middle of all this stress he started to wonder what life was all about, or maybe was it because of all the relentless stress, it made him question his very being.

All he knew was that he was no longer the bright positive person he used to be. He had become totally identified by work. He had become just another Domain worker, a dispensable Domain worker. His personality had changed. No longer Old Snoz, who the kids flocked to for sweets or the apothecary their parents respected for his self-attained knowledge and special caring way.

Snoz also shared with them that his original identity, that bright, quick-witted centre of his family, friends and work friends had, over time, been diluted down to a wishy-washy copy of his former self through work. Now he had no time for his family, he rarely visited his aged parents and his long-suffering wife just sighed to herself at what life used to be like living with him. His children had long since stopped asking him to take them out to play and just carried on with life on their own. His friends didn't welcome him or want to be in his company because now he only talked about work, incessantly complaining about the Domain Apothecary, he had no other conversation.

Everything seemed futile; everything he did under this new regime seemed such a waste of time. Snoz told them that he was 'burning out' but hadn't recognised it in himself, neither did he afford himself any recovery periods. At the time, he believed there must be more to life than what he was doing, there just must, but he didn't know what it was or where to find it. He had completely and utterly burnt out. He was off work and, at first, in a daze for weeks.

There was long pause before he said: "What is amazing is the fact that I have never told anyone else how I felt until today. I believed I was the only person in the world who ever felt like this, I believed I was the only one in the world who couldn't cope and had failed like this." What he went on to share made them even more uncomfortable especially Lord Seren: "I also believed that had I sought help from the Domain Apothecary whilst I was burning out it would have been seen as a sign of weakness. Any admission of, 'not being able to cope', would have been tantamount to committing apothecary Hara-Kiri."

He finished by saying: "Now, in the autumn years of my life it looks to the outside world that I have slowed down and I'm taking life at a more pedestrian pace. Some folk even think I've become lazy, but my current pace of work ironically is achieving far more than I ever achieved during my 'bad times' or when I was working 'normally', before my bad times. I learned salutary lessons from the experience and have become so much more organised and productive. I'm even more sensitive now to the needs of my customers than ever before."

As he left them Snoz felt a great weight had been lifted off his shoulders. It was as though he had confessed that he had completely burnt out. He left them a happier man.

The four were silent, each recognising the parallels with Floot's situation.

FLOOTNOTE:
Leaders admitting they can't cope is like committing career Hara-Kiri in some cultures

Chapter Three - Part Two

THREE LEADERS BURNING OUT

(TINK THE DEALER)

'Relentlessly ambitious' was the best way to describe Tink; ambitious in the extreme and personally driven to the detriment of everything else in his life. But right now, as he sat in front of them, he wasn't twitching to get back out there and do more business as soon as possible as the four of them had predicted. Tink sat opposite them with not a hint of stress on his face, listened to their request and calmly recounted his tale.

His brightly coloured clothes mirrored his demeanour. Bright blue trousers, bright green waistcoat, bright orange jacket, a bright red spotted scarf and a bright wide smile.

Tink admitted to them he had been a workaholic; he loved the cut and thrust of buying and selling, finding every opportunity to make a shilling. He loved the feel of the win, especially the win. It was infectious; it drove him straight on to the next challenge. Every day he loved the hunt and the 'kill' in his trading world. His world had been fun with its ups and downs and he liked nothing more than to drop into bed, tired out but content, accompanied by a superb feeling of personal achievement. He enjoyed his reputation as being one of the most successful dealers in Ten-Tree-Wood; a reputation earned through hard work.

Tink's work ethic had come from his parents who had both worked all their lives in much harsher circumstances. They never stopped trading, every day was a new challenge to them and as travelling folk they needed to make a shilling wherever they were, for they were always moving. Goodness only knew when they would be able to make another shilling. They had been his role models.

Tink lived on his own and, despite the remonstrations of his saddened parents he had given up the travelling life and now owned a modern house. His home was comfortable for a bachelor and he surrounded himself with every modern, got to have, gismo going. He recalled that he had quickly surpassed anything his parents ever owned or dreamed of owning, but this wasn't enough for him and his ambition drove him harder and harder. He said he felt on fire with the buzz of success. He couldn't wait to get up in the mornings and start a new day.

Tink's way of life gradually changed as he became more successful. He moved from working on his own to having three people working for him. With staff, he needed more stock to provide the greater turnover. More stock required warehouses. Employing folk brought its own problems and it wasn't long before he needed folk to manage the folk he was employing. He then needed folk to maintain the buildings needed to house the increased number of folk who were working for him and the classic downward spiral had begun. But he believed he was coping, he believed it was just a blip and things would get better soon. He just needed to work harder.

He went on to explain to the ardent faces before him: "In life, as you run a business, you are continually learning. You learn what sells and you buy more. You learn what doesn't sell and buy less. In the middle of all this pressure you'd have thought I'd have had the time to stop and say to myself this isn't working I must do something different before it's too late. In the middle of all this pace I learned nothing, nothing at all.

"My parents' simple, successful business model of making a shilling on ten things every day was better than my current business model of hanging on to things for a year to maybe make 2 shillings. My business model patently wasn't working but I couldn't see it, I believed I just needed to work harder and longer and raise my performance."

Tink outlined how he was working all hours to pay the rent for the warehouses to store his stock to generate the turnover. He worked evenings and weekends to make enough money to pay the wages of the folk he employed. He drove himself harder and longer but achieved less and less. Consequently, over a long period of time, things slowly started to go downhill. His list of creditors became longer, his stock was shrinking as more folk refused him credit and fewer folk wanted to do business with him.

He went on to tell the four of them he wasn't able to relax and as a result became more and more tired, he seemed unable to recover, whatever he did. Alongside the tiredness he experienced an uncharacteristic lack of confidence. He couldn't concentrate or focus on any one thing but kept starting new projects without finishing the last. No longer was he the life and soul of the party, but started shutting his friends and family out. He just didn't have the patience for them and they were politely shunning him for all he talked about was work. He also started complaining about constant lower back pain, persistent headaches and always seemed to have a cold.

Then came the tipping point. One day, after a blisteringly busy few weeks, he needed help to keep up his relentless work regime. His help came in the form of a bottle. From that day on alcohol, that had once only accompanied holidays and celebrations, became his everyday way of life. He drank to sleep, he drank to work, he drank to be creative and to relax he drank. Tink explained this had been a time he never wanted to return to and found it embarrassing even talking about it. He drank more to keep going. He drank more to stop worrying. His business model was flawed. He realised his bottomless appetite for more and more money was killing him and this lack of buzz from personal accomplishment was eating at his very soul.

The day he found himself borrowing money from his simple parents to pay the wages of his employees was a conscience-jangling wake-up call. Here he was, with all the trappings of so-called success, working every hour of the day and night, needing to be bailed out of trouble by his parents who had worked so hard for their simple way of life.

He was completely and utterly burnt out! And being burnt out was not a 'badge of honour'. Tink explained that burning out was an addictive behaviour but unlike other addictive behaviours there was no stigma until it was too late!

Tink became thoughtful for a minute and his audience kept quiet in deference to his story.

He said having hit rock bottom, he realised it was up to him to stop, choose to change and then change. He no longer drank to keep going; now he only drank socially. He had turned his work life around and could say with certainty that he was happy. Most importantly, he had realigned his life aspirations. The process of protecting his people, shutting down his business and realigning his life aspirations had taken about six, liberating months.

He enquired if this was what they had wanted to hear and they answered in unison that it was exactly what they feared. There were many similarities between Tink's tale and what they were watching with Floot.

Flootnote: Early in our careers we can drink more than we can afford. Now we can afford more than we can drink

Flootnote: Do. Or do not. There is no try

Chapter Three - Part Three

THREE LEADERS BURNING OUT

(DAI-BONES THE UNDERTAKER)

Walking at his traditional funeral gait, Dai-Bones shuffled into the meeting room, sat down and took off his tall, felt, funeral hat complete with its black lace bow. As he placed his big hat on the table it was as if he parked his solemn respectful face inside it and what was beneath was transformed into a huge smile. With big, shiny, white teeth and bright eyes that were alive with life he asked the assembled four: "Now, how can I help?" They were taken aback and embarrassed that they had compartmentalised him by his profession despite the tell-tale whiff of embalming fluid in the air.

Barley thanked him for coming and explained that they had been observing Floot's behaviour and come to the conclusion that he was 'burning out', hence the reason for the very secret meeting. Barley also suggested a level of discretion and secrecy was required after the meeting as they were dealing with a very sensitive issue.

Dai-Bones listened intently, was silent for nearly a minute and then he put his hands in the air and exploded: "But, you three are the problem! By not confronting Floot's behaviour you're the real problem! You've demonstrated that to everyone in Ten-Tree-Wood. 'Shhhhhhhh, It's a secret'." And with that Dai-Bones put his finger to his lips and looked furtively first over one shoulder then over his other shoulder: "No! It's not a secret. By treating Floot's behaviour as a secret you are the very ones who are compounding the problem. You are perpetuating an issue which, had you tackled it sensitively when it first manifested itself, would have been eminently solvable. Do you think there is anyone in Ten-Tree-Wood who doesn't know that Floot is not himself?"

The trio of senior managers shuffled uncomfortably in their chairs at the challenge and Lord Seren accepted the criticism of his complicity, silently.

Calmer now from his exasperation, he continued: "Everybody knows, absolutely everybody knows. The whole community is talking about Floot. The problem is not, that nobody takes any notice of leaders like Floot but it's the exact opposite. Everyone is continually watching his behaviour. They all know Floot is that amazing leader who transformed this community from a 'bottom of the pile' place to live to a place of 'first choice'. Of course everyone knows he's not himself. Believe me, you're the only ones who are not talking openly about it. And with a crooked index finger pointed accusingly at the four of them saying slowly, "You're the problem."

Their embarrassment could be heard in the silence.

Fortunately, Dai-Bones broke the silence: "Let me tell you what happened to me. I was happy as Larry as Ten-Tree-Wood's undertaker. I lived in a lovely house with my wife and two children who I love dearly and I have much to be thankful for. I worked hard and was proud of the 'send-offs' I arranged for folk on their way to the big Woodland Community in the sky."

"My coffins were pieces of furniture, hand-made by me and my team with the same care we would build into a chest of drawers. If I do say it myself, our coffins were too good to be put in the ground; somehow they should have been on display for longer than just a week."

"Folk came to me from miles around passing several other coffin-makers on the way. The wall of my workshop is papered with all the certificates we won for joinery and I pinned up all the letters of thanks I received from the relatives of our customers. I was proud of my little five-person business and what I had achieved. I was alive and I felt invincible."

"Then came the very long harsh winter two years ago. There had been surges of demands on my skills in bad winters before, but nothing like this. Folk were dying everywhere. How could I turn their relatives away? I felt their grief, I felt their pain, I couldn't turn them away. Many of these folk were my friends."

"My coffins were part of their closure so I was emotionally involved in every funeral. The demands on my feelings were exhausting but whatever happened I couldn't let these lovely folk down. I told them we would manage somehow."

"I thought I could cope by cutting some corners, small things at first. We started to build coffins at night on overtime to cope with the demand. I suggested we build them on a 'one-size fits all' model. My workmen were dead against it at first but I insisted. It helped me address the volume problem, but I was becoming grumpier, more intolerant and blind to what I was doing."

"First, one of my loyal team left then another saying that they didn't like the way the business was going. Then the last two left. I brought casual labour in to see me through but it didn't work. Because folk saw me desperately trying to cope on my own they independently decided it wasn't fair to say anything, exactly as you are doing with Floot. If they weren't complaining about the quality then I could reasonably assume they must be OK with what I was producing; the classic **Quality/Acceptance Nexus (Awbery).** So, I produced more of the same and cut even more corners. Nobody said anything to me about the quality so I carried on."

"All through my business life I have sought ways to improve what I was doing. I had always applied that learning and hence became a better and more professional craftsman throughout the whole of my career, but in the middle of this 'bad time' I was too close to the problem to see what was happening. I was systematically undoing all the years of learning in my trade and my work became no better than when I first started as a coffin-maker. I look back and I'm ashamed,

I'm totally ashamed of the work I was turning out. My only excuse is, I had become totally drained of all my emotions."

"Then one day I was accompanying a coffin and heard some comments about the quality of my craftsmanship, coming from a little boy. His comments shook me to the core. It was the best thing that could have happened to me. I knew I had to stop right then and put my life back in order. I finished the day, put on my coat, switched off the lights in my workshop, locked up and went home for about three months when I did precisely nothing."

"I was absolutely burnt out. I couldn't even visit my empty workshop. I couldn't think straight, I couldn't communicate properly. If it hadn't been for my wonderful wife I don't know how I would have coped."

"The community managed well enough by importing coffins to see them through and the world didn't implode. The community carried on as normal. Folk still went shopping, carts rumbled past my house, market day was as busy as it ever was and life just went on as it always had. I was angry at first. I felt there should be some acknowledgment from them of how low I had become, some display of sympathy or regret. After all, I had crashed trying to meet their needs but to them it was as though nothing had happened, the community had regrouped without me and life carried on. I wasn't that important after all!"

"I'm OK now. I've cleared out all that anger stuff now; it wasn't their fault it was totally mine. Life is in perspective, two of my old team are back with me and we only accept work when we are sure we can do it to the quality we did before my 'bad times'."

With that, Dai-Bones replaced his hat and his undertaker's solemn face, bade them all goodnight and left the silent group to their own levels of embarrassment. The meeting broke up in silence, three of them lost in their own thoughts and Lord Seren wondering if the current damage being caused by the new Domain Queen was recoverable?

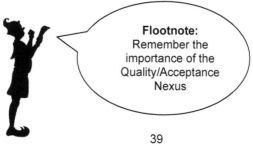

Floatnote:
Remember the importance of the Quality/Acceptance Nexus

Chapter Four

WHAT HAVE WE FOUND OUT SO FAR?

The following evening the four met up again and Barley called them to order.

Dai-Full-Pelt broke the solemn mood: "So what have we found out so far?"

Dandelion started: "Before they burnt out, Snoz, Tink and Dai-Bones were all on fire in their businesses and enjoying life. (Fredenberger). All three were recognised as high performers by their peers. Their pressures were building up over time but they didn't recognise they were burning out until the situation was too late. No-one else took their situation in hand and talked to them about the unsustainability of what they were doing. We must learn from this."

Lord Seren nodded sagely: "Don't forget that some cases of burnout are as a result of a break down in home relationships or home circumstances. The symptoms may well be the same as work-related symptoms, but the cause might be quite different. Leaders need to mindful of this possibility when observing gradual changes in the performance of members of their team. Equally important is the fact that burnout effects all levels of leader from team leader up to corporate leader. It is not selective only of senior leaders but will also manifest itself upon junior leaders. "

Barley nodded then took over: "From all three we have listened to, it's apparent that burnout was definitely job-related, whether it was driven by processes, targets or line-leadership style. All three seemed to suffer a feeling of powerlessness to change. So while the organisation or circumstances set the environment for burnout, it was the way the leader chose to respond to it that determined if they burnt out or not. None of the three stopped and regrouped, they all believed they were powerless to change. Their only response was to increase their work rate by working longer hours."

"With Old Snoz the situation was the change of boss, with Tink it was to keep the business going and his genuine social responsibility towards his employees and with Dai-Bones the situation was the harsh winter and his genuine emotional responsibility towards his customers. Each of them admitted they had not learned from the experience by adapting their behaviour when the pressure was building. Their only solution was to put in more hours."

Lord Seren interjected: "My research from the animal world uncovered the need for good health to survive today's pressures, a level of maturity to learn from the experience and regular, protected time to recover from stress. If any one of these is absent then coping with pressure/stress is far more difficult."

Dai-Full-Pelt took up from Lord Seren: "It's apparent that they were all suffering from what was relentless pressure. Normal everyday stress is a parabolic occurrence and each of them has adapted to, and recovered from, changing environments and circumstantial stresses a dozen times before. However, when they were burning out through relentless pressures and higher targets, they all had 'delusions about their own capability' (Casserly and Megginson) and believed by working longer hours they were coping. In each case, complete burnout came from unremitting workloads, time pressures, volume or inadequate staffing."

Barley continued: "So, there are two driving forces for burnout. (Casserly and Megginson). 1. Work took over their worlds to the exclusion of everything else and 2. They all lost their own identity and became identified solely by work. Each displayed a complete failure to be reflexive, learn from their experiences and change things."

"In the end, complete burnout manifested itself with all of them as severe exhaustion and distress at being overwhelmed at work and it took between three months and a year to recover."

"May I share my explanation of where I think the three of them are at present?"

With that Lord Seren drew his diagram on the table.

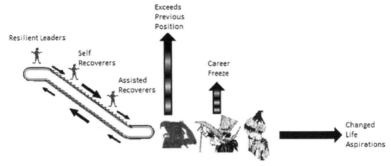

Old Snoz Dai-Bones Tink

He explained that the figure at the top of the escalator was one of those leaders who were able to cope with the rise and fall of stress and recovered regularly. He called these RESILIENT LEADERS.

He explained that some leaders travelled a third of the way down the escalator before they realised what was happening to them. At this point they were able to get off the escalator unassisted, change the way they were leading to become a 'SELF RECOVERER' returning back up to the top. However, by this point there is a noticeable reduction in their performance.

Lord Seren continued to explain the 'ASSISTED RECOVERERS' position at two-thirds of the way down the escalator, the serious deterioration in the leader's performance and the need for a 'Recovery Buddy'.

Then he went on to describe the three leaders with complete burnout at the bottom i.e. Tink, Dai-Bones and Snoz. "These three completely burnt out, were unable to function properly and unable to undertake any meaningful work for a period of time."

"From their tales I believe Tink has completely changed his life aspirations and is now content. I believe Dai-Bones has repositioned his goals, become a realist and accepted a career freeze having downsized his business. And Old Snoz has recovered completely, having learned huge lessons from the experience and returned to his position at the top of the escalator without succumbing to any lasting problems as a result of the stresses of being completely burnt out. I believe he is capable of much more. All three of them are heroes in my eyes."

Dai-Full-Pelt made a solemn observation: "If we had lost any of them completely, Snoz, Tink or Dai-Bones, our community here in Ten-Tree-Wood would have been the poorer. We would have lost three good folk who were all offering superb services. The challenge would be to find folk of their calibre very quickly. I'm embarrassed we didn't know this was happening under our very noses. How does Ten-Tree-Wood appear to the other communities? Imagine the banners."

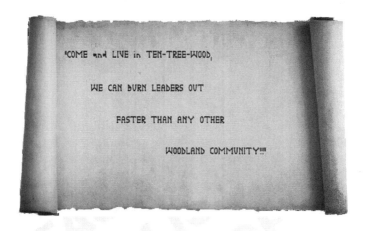

It was Dandelion who asked the obvious question: "Lord Seren, do you think Floot is completely burnt out and at the bottom of the escalator?"

"No, I believe Floot is two-thirds of the way down and needs a 'Recovery Buddy' to help him off the escalator and together they would formulate his recovery strategy. The skills of a 'Recovery Buddy' are similar to a coach, however, a 'Recovery Buddy' will also have studied the recovery strategies of other leaders suffering from burnout and be able to apply a mix of coaching and mentoring techniques."

"The 'Recovery Buddy' also has a responsibility to help the leader re-orientate their work/life balance, so some knowledge of health and wellbeing is also helpful. If the three of you believe I could help, and Floot is agreeable, I would be pleased to offer my assistance as his 'Recovery Buddy'. However, you need to have the very difficult conversation with him first."

Barley thanked Lord Seren for his help, finishing thoughtfully with: "It begs the question how many more folk are burning out in the Domain?"

"I fear there are many, many."

Flootnote:
Burning out is not a badge of honour

Chapter Five

THE PHYSIOLOGICAL ASPECTS OF BURNOUT

The next day the four met again. "What physiological things are happening to Floot?" asked Barley. "What are the warning signs we ought to be looking for to enable us to recognise when it happens to someone else? What can we learn from all this?"

"Well, Floot's lost his libido and that's a certainty!" Bluntly announced Dandelion making the other two look up at her at exactly the same time in an enquiring manner and Lord Seren spluttered over his cup of tea spilling it everywhere.

"Not me!" she snapped at them. "Surely you must have noticed every time he passes a pretty face he becomes all excited and the bell on his hat rings uncontrollably? Don't tell me you haven't seen it happen? That's why he snatches his hat off as soon as he sees a pretty face. He's not being gallant, he's super excited by a pretty face and doesn't want to be embarrassed by his bell ringing for all it's worth."

"Well, only the other day, the prettiest marsh fairy walked passed him and smiled the loveliest smile and in his burned out state she might just as well have been a Troll. Not a tinkle, not a ding nor a dong. That's got to be one of the symptoms of burnout."

"Any other signs?" asked Dai-Full-Pelt, tut-tutting to himself and raising his eyes to the ceiling.

"Yes, sleep deprivation or interrupted sleep patterns," said Barley.

"As a badger I'm often unable to sleep at night so I take a stroll around the village. I often see Floot's light on and he's working late into the night. If he isn't working, he is having a few drinks to help him sleep. In the morning, he seems to need a big slug of parsnip wine to get him started. He says, 'it's for medicinal purposes,' but I think he does it most days."

"Have you said anything to him?"

"No."

Tink the dealer's story flashed through all their minds at the same time, of how Tink needed alcohol to start the day, to be creative and at the end of the day to help him sleep.

"Anything else?"

"Yes, he is always complaining about his bad back. When he gets out of a chair it's as if he's a hundred years old. I've also heard him complain about his stiff neck and headaches and he's putting on weight from all the rubbish food he's eating for quickness. The fairies can't let his trousers out anymore, they're at maximum and his shirt is stretched that tight over his tummy if a button comes off it will kill someone."

Dandelion suggested another symptom: "He can't let go. He was supposed to have a week's holiday instead; he spent the whole time checking in on things on his Pix-e-mails. It's a really bad sign when your only company for breakfast, lunch or dinner are your Pix-e-mails. I don't think he was away from here for more than a couple of hours and when I challenged him on it, as you would expect me to, he just said it was, 'his form of relaxation'. He's demonstrating a type of martyr behaviour, anxious all of the time, a cliff edge culture. He seems to be a victim now not the old, strong-willed Floot we all knew and loved.

"We've already said he's forever got a cold because of his reduced immune system and also he's always at the apothecary for medicine to settle his tummy."

"So, Floot has lost his libido, isn't sleeping, is drinking more than normal, is putting on weight, has a bad back, is suffering from headaches, can't let go, is forever checking his Pix-e-mails at meal times and has a severely reduced immune system, quite a catalogue. But do you know the worst thing I've observed as Floot burns out," said Lord Seren with despondency in his voice, "is his reduced memory function, asking the same questions over and over again, not remembering what he went upstairs for and when he sees you he's forgotten why he needed to talk to you. I'm afraid it may point to premature senescence unless he changes his behaviour."

This comment really made them sit up.

Dai-Full-Pelt went on to say: "Our next step is to get Snoz, Tink and Dai-Bones back and find out what they did to recover from their ordeals."

Flootnote: Farmer: "I had just trained my donkey to manage without food and water when it dropped down dead. Who'd have thought it?"

Chapter Six

THE RECOVERY STRATEGIES OF THREE BURNED OUT LEADERS

The next evening Snoz, Tink and Dai-Bones sat in front of the three senior managers and Lord Seren, each having willingly agreed to share their stories and provide their audience with a chance to explore the differences in their recovery strategies.

Snoz the apothecary began: "One day, during the three months I was off work recovering, I took it upon myself to go off into the wood and just think. While I was there I asked myself some questions. Was what I was being asked to do impossible or just difficult? Was what I was being asked to do difficult or just different? Had I become so set in my ways that I now painted everything the Domain Apothecary suggested as black, regardless? Was I unhappy, and if I couldn't change the situation could I change the way I felt about it? In fact did I want to change at all?

I came to the conclusion that what I was being asked to do was just different not difficult, I didn't even listen to the Domain Apothecary anymore to decide if he was right or wrong and no, I wasn't happy, and yes, I could change the way I felt about it and finally yes, I did want to change."

Snoz shared with them that even after his soul searching walk in the woods it had still taken several months of phased return to work to reorganise himself working smarter and in a more organised way. He also programmed into his week, complete recovery periods away from work. Every time he returned from a complete absence from work he recounted to them that he returned with a new vim and vigour for work, new ideas and renewed enthusiasm. He translated the negative burnout experience into positive personal development and gradually improved.

It took several attempts making positive suggestions to the Domain Apothecary before he noticed any changes in their relationship. He felt the main turning point came when the Domain Apothecary asked for his advice. Snoz said he believed he had turned himself around. Now life was good. Life had purpose again. He was back doing more in less time with better results for his one and a half communities than ever before.

"One thing I stopped doing in the bad times," said Snoz, "is collecting all my own herbs from the woods. I used to walk miles and miles but I stopped because I thought it was taking me too long and so I started buying them in. Now I walk in the woods every day. For about an hour I walk and think in my own silent space as I collect my herbs. It prepares me for the day, it cuts out all the 'noise', it calms any anxieties about working with difficult people and it charges my batteries. It has also restored my fitness level."

Snoz continued: "Now I have climbed back from my negatively changed personality to my old self again. I'm now who I was and I think I'm known again as lovably Old Snoz which is the best recovery benefit of all.

"I also feel able to share some good news with you all. I have just been nominated to become the new Central Domain Apothecary as the current apothecary is moving on."

All six congratulated Old Snoz on his appointment and told him it had been well-earned.

Lord Seren nodded knowingly.

***

Tink went second: "The thought of making the folk who had helped build my empire redundant was appalling to me. They had given me their all and some of them were working as hard as I was to keep the business going."

"They worked long hours; they worked at weekends and did far more than they were ever originally employed to or, in fact, more than I paid them to. How could I live with myself if the business went under?"

"However, soon after my conscience–jangling requirement to borrow money from my parents to pay the wages of my team I had an epiphany. Without doubt, I realised I was going to physically collapse, maybe die leaving all the problems I'd caused for my ageing parents and my depleted business team to sort out without me. That was totally unacceptable. I took a couple of months off to start recovering and, when well enough, made some plans."

Tink suggested to them that it was like slipping a yoke off his shoulders when he made the decision to stop trading, give up all his stock and the team who constituted his empire. He vowed he wouldn't let any of his people down and when well enough, set about helping every one of them find another job and now they had all been placed. Finding jobs had been a real challenge but he felt really good about his success.

As he began to recover Tink explained, he removed from his life all the things he didn't need but came to believe he couldn't do without, such as the big house, the drink and the gismos.

Once again he became contented with life, set himself realistic goals every day and celebrated little successes. Through the bad times he had piled on loads of weight which made him sluggish, he didn't think quickly, he slept badly, the alcohol made him feel rough every morning and he became puffed out climbing stairs. He had become ridiculously neglectful of his health and well-being. Tink explained how he set about living sensibly again, looking after his health and with a little exercise every day quickly returned to his trim shape.

Tink patted his lean tummy. He declared he was pleased with his slim figure and felt good about himself. He went on to say that folk told him his eyes were bright and he had become fun to be with again.

He no longer held his head in his hands, neither did he sigh at everything.

He went on to say that there was no way he could have continued at that pace and in his case a radical change of job was necessary. Coupled with a new eating and living regime he now felt great, really great. He didn't expand on how dark his world had become as his reliance on alcohol had developed. Perhaps it was because he believed he would never revisit that level of dependency on anything again.

He shared with them his personal development: "I learned to handle work targets and put them in perspective in my life. Now I believe I have re-established my self-esteem and once again I have become happy with lots of small, but very real, personal accomplishments. My life aspirations have all changed."

***

Dai-Bones had listened intently to the proceedings then said: "Oh, how I wish I had known about you two while I was going through my 'bad time'. I so needed to talk to someone because it wasn't until I confessed to you four," nodding at Dai-Full-Pelt, Barley, Dandelion and Lord Seren, "that I realised I hadn't articulated how I felt to anyone."

"I admit after being here I went home and I cried. I cried because you had shown me that it was OK to burnout. I wasn't the only one. There were folk as good and well-respected as Snoz and Tink and Floot suffering from burning out. I felt so much better."

"During the 'bad' times I had become drained of all my emotions and struggled to recover on my own. My wife was amazing and so caring, but how much quicker would I have recovered if there had been someone there to talk to who had been on the same journey as me?"

"When was my turning point? Well I'll tell you. One day as I was walking slowly in front of the cortège I overheard a little pixie boy say that he could see his grandad's arm hanging out of the coffin. I saw that some of the nails had come out of the side and there was a gap in the coffin. The little boy then said to his brother that, 'he had spent more care making his dog's kennel!' I was devastated."

"That was my wake up call."

"It took a little pixie boy to tell me that what I was producing wasn't good enough. Nobody was big enough or brave enough except this little pixie boy. Everybody was keeping the problem a secret. They were all putting up with my poor standards and poor workmanship and accepting it."

"Poor quality had slowly crept up on me and I wasn't aware of anything. I was using inferior quality timber, I was using nails instead of screws, I wasn't finishing the coffins very well and just painting the occupant's name on the lids instead of carving them."

"If only the first time I had cut corners someone had said: 'Sorry, that's not good enough for my loved one', I would have been so embarrassed and immediately would have made a better job or put my hand up and told my boss, the Domain Coffin-Maker, I needed extra help which would have had to come from another community."

"But they didn't and the result was terrible. What you three are doing is the same. You're putting up with poor service and behaviour from Floot. You're not complaining or giving him any constructive feedback so he can assume you are OK with his new behaviour."

"Remember the **Quality/Acceptance Nexus**. We all have a responsibility to give constructive feedback to our teams, our bosses and our suppliers.

"Fortunately for me, the community imported coffins whilst I was off work and eventually the weather improved."

"I also had time to start looking after myself again. I stopped calling in for pies and chips every day to save going home to eat and now I walk everywhere rather than take the cart. My clothes fit again and it doesn't take three or four goes to buckle my belt in the last hole. I thought with all the extra work I'd get fitter but I didn't, I got fatter. I was eating rubbish, fast food. Now I'm back and feel good, I feel like I used to. It makes so much difference."

"But one thing is certain; I'll never go back to being burnt out again. I've learned that lesson the hard way. On my personal development journey I have learned to call for help or turn work down rather than revert back to those days. I've now set myself a limit on what I can do to a very high standard in a reasonable week to retain my reputation. From now on I'll position myself by price rather than volume."

The four looked at each other following these profound thoughts from this simple undertaker.

Snoz, Tink and Dai-Bones left together as new friends having survived the common adversity.

***

"So what have we found out?" asked Dandelion.

"Snoz, Tink and Dai-Bones are all contented now but they would all have recovered much quicker and not have fallen so low if folk had been honest with them early on. We as senior managers of the organisation have a huge responsibility to recognise leaders in trouble at an early stage, be honest with them and intervene."

"Snoz reorganised his workload, set about developing a better relationship with his boss and now has been promoted. Tink accepted that the business model he had built was not working and made radical changes to his life aspirations and Dai-Bones has chosen and frozen the size of his business."

"Now it's time to find out what the best communities are doing to combat this terrible waste of talent," said Barley.

Flootnote: The most important thing organisations can do is look at the workloads and targets of its leaders and ask: 'Honestly is this a realistic expectation?'

Chapter Seven

BENCHMARKING BURNOUT PREVENTION STRATEGIES

In traditional Ten-Tree-Wood management style the three of them set off to find out what the best of the best Domains were doing to protect their woodland leaders from burning out. They used their management networks (**Pixie Dust III**) to understand where to look first. Lord Seren said he would contribute by visiting the best of the best of the 'Big People's' organisations but, with a twinkle in his eye, suggested he probably wouldn't be long.

Barley travelled to a community in the Northern Domain.

Here she discovered from the Community that they believed leaders burning out had a direct correlation with leader's health and wellbeing. Those in good health and wellbeing were less likely to burnout. As such, the topic had rocketed to the top of the agenda of the Community Senior Leadership Team because they had already considered a number of 'what if certain leaders burnout' scenarios and what they discovered made them very uncomfortable. Now that they had started to look closely, they discovered there were several leaders in various stages of burning out. The workload of the leaders who had already burnt out had already been distributed around the surviving leaders, further compounding the problem.

The Senior Leadership Team believed the 'do nothing strategy' for their community was unsustainable. The whole community was on a downward spiral of health and wellbeing and some community leaders completely burning out would be inevitable. What the Senior Leadership Team needed to do became blindingly obvious.

They surveyed all the folk in the community and quickly discovered that their population profile was ageing and, as old age never came alone, it was accompanied by a plethora of health problems. Their research showed them that 1 in 5 of their folk were already obese, 1 in 6 folk were already suffering mental health problems, the number of folk with diabetes was rocketing and the incidence of their folk who had work-related muscular-skeletal problems and arthritis through work was rising steadily (AXA PPP Health).

Some of the folk who lived in the community were at risk from several illnesses at the same time. What the Senior Leadership Team found from their research was that the incidence of high blood pressure, poor diet, sedentary behaviour, stress and alcohol abuse could, in many cases, be reversed by education. It was evident to the Senior Leadership Team that health education was not being adequately practised at home so they decided they would reinforce it when their folk were at work.

The Senior Leadership Team changed their perspective on their woodland folk, no longer seeing them just as workers but as whole people who, if encouraged to improve their health and wellbeing, would bring new life into the workplace and reverse the catastrophic waste of leadership talent.

What the Community also discovered, Barley found out, was that as blood pressure and other illnesses increased, so cognitive performance deteriorated (Sing Manaux). As all the Domain economies were moving from a 'grunt and muscle' economy to a far more technically driven economy, consistent, cognitive performance was becoming an imperative. Demonstrating that the community had the capability to become a serious player was essential for their very existence.

A further driver of the strategy of the community was money. For example, the Senior Leadership Team was convinced if they improved the health and well-being of the folk who worked in their community then absence from work, caused by leaders burning out amongst other things, would fall. The overall absence rate was currently running at about 10%, meaning, out of the 100 jobs necessary to maintain the community, there were always at least ten folk off sick for some reason or other. That meant they employed 110 folk to do 100 jobs. Ten folk came in as temporary workers and leadership talent from other communities at enhanced wages. If the Senior Leadership Team could drop this absence to 5% by their health and well-being strategy then they could save the enhanced wages of five temporary staff.

An additional positive monetary outcome would be the improved cognitive performance of their folk, enhancing their ability to compete in the new technological economy.

Barley believed that by improving the health and well-being of the folk in Ten-Tree-Wood, as the Northern Community had achieved, could breathe new life into her community and go some way towards combatting the current burnout culture. She returned to report her findings.

***

Dandelion went to a Community in the Southern Domain. Here she found that the Senior Leadership Team had identified leaders burning out as one of their most urgent challenges. They decided to embed a coaching and mentoring culture as part of their strategy to reverse this trend. By establishing a regular series of interventions it was found by the Senior Leadership Team, that early recognition of leader burnout was identified.

To Dandelion there seemed to be two strands to their coaching and mentoring strategy. The first was the early identification of those leaders at risk from burning out and secondly, to see coaching and mentoring as a talent acceleration proposition (CIPD).

The Senior Leadership Team saw coaching and mentoring as 'enabling people to improve' (Zeus and Skiffington) and interpreted the word 'improve' as enabling leaders who were burning out to design their own recovery strategy. On the other hand, 'enabling people to improve' immeasurably augmented the learning of those who were coping. The Senior Leadership Team believed they already had a cohort of 'wise' leaders as coaches who, like Mentor in Greek Mythology, could 'teach them all they knew'.

They had angst over whether to apply a coaching culture or a mentoring culture, realising that neither could stand alone; there being occasions when both approaches should be used in the same conversation. They adopted the technique of Menching, (Awbery/Asset Skills) a combination of using knowledge and skills (mentoring) and developmental questioning and feedback (coaching) to encourage individuals to challenge their own thoughts and provide their own solutions enabling them to improve.

The Southern Community Senior Leadership Team identified that the most critical factor for creating a successful coaching culture was the total commitment of senior levels of leadership. They ensured that the coaching and mentoring strategy supported the talent strategy and linked to the Community business objectives. They then embedded the new coaching and mentoring culture within an already established culture of empowerment and continuous improvement culture selling it to the whole community as a developmental tool rather than a remedial tool.

Finally, the Senior Leadership Team deliberated long and hard on the critical task of pairing and matching coaches to coachees and mentors to mentees.

The Team shared with Dandelion that a spin-off advantage had become evident, namely the improvement in the performance of the coaches and mentors as well as the individuals being coached and mentored. What Dandelion also found amazing was that, whereas the strategy had originally been established for protection against leader's burnout and the development of other leaders, these coachees, seeing its power first hand, had in turn become practitioners of Menching with their own teams. The culture was being cascaded down through the organisation; the ultimate success.

***

Dai-Full-Pelt went to a Community in the Western Domain discovering a community that had successfully implemented a health and well-being culture purely for the benefit of the folk who lived there. There had been no hidden agenda, no covert plan and it was not a turn-around strategy. What had been there from the start of the initiative were two 'white knights' as they were called, who cared passionately about the deterioration in the health and well-being of their community. Two white knights who had watched leaders at all levels burning out so took it upon themselves to make a difference.

These 'white knights' were two ordinary folk who believed they could raise the engagement of the community in its health and wellbeing. Two folk who believed they could transform their community to become a community of first choice, recruiting the very best talent and contributing to its future prosperity. And they had done it. They had dispelled the negativity, encouraged, cajoled and finally engaged the input from the community Senior Leadership Team right down to the youngest members of their society and their enthusiasm for success had been infectious.

Now there was a waiting list of folk who wanted to come to live in their Community, there was reduced absence at work, early recognition of leaders burning out without blame or retribution, no queues at the apothecary and there were examples of best social practice everywhere.

One unexpected advantage of this health and well-being culture in their Community was that, whereas in other communities there was a huge turnover of dissatisfied, middle leaders all hunting for better jobs where the grass was perceived to be greener, here in their Community there was a markedly reduced turnover of middle leaders.

A genuine social community strategy driven by just two 'white knights' who, it must be pointed out, had other full-time jobs.

Here is a list of some of the ideas implemented over a two-year period focussing on folk helping themselves and folk helping others…

My Health…

1. Weight management programme with personal trainers
2. Breakfast wellness clinics
3. Food swap campaigns
4. Sleep clinic
5. Stress audits
6. Healthy cooking lessons
7. Walking groups
8. Hydration campaigns
9. Health screenings
10. Mindfulness and meditation

Health of Others…

1. Mental health awareness training
2. Talking buddies
3. Give something back – volunteering
4. Give blood

5. First-aid training
6. Reiki

Wherever Dai-Full-Pelt went in the community ideas were being put forward to improve things, not necessarily from the leaders, but by everyone. There was a hum about the community to be better not only for the wellbeing of individuals but also for the betterment of the whole community. He hadn't experienced this before. Here were a range of ideas that could be implemented back home in Ten-Tree-Wood.

***

Lord Seren returned from visiting the Big People's organisations and, contrary to his original derogatory remarks, some good ideas were forthcoming. He found out that when leaders completely burnt out organisations were faced by a number of serious issues.

Firstly, in the Big People's world the law was on the side of Duty of Care, negligent employers could become liable for debilitating work-related stress. This was a real wake up call. How would his Domain fare? Not well he surmised.

Secondly, if organisations disregard leaders who were burning out they faced long periods of leader absence, redistribution of the leaders' workloads and prolonged anger about the organisation, brand and reputation. Lord Seren had never considered brand or reputation to be an issue previously, however, if a talent war for leaders started, brand and reputation would influence potential leader's perception of an organisation being an 'employer of first choice' or otherwise. In a talent war, brand and reputation would be of immense importance.

Thirdly, all the research indicated that those talking on 'hands-free' telephones when driving their Big People's carts had worse reaction times than those over the legal limit of alcohol. Therefore, how could organisations expect team members to work and drive at the same time? Despite all the compelling research, nobody wanted to rehearse how to explain to a junior leader's widow or widower that senior leaders had expected them to be able to drive a cart and take important work calls even on a hands-free phone.

What Lord Seren discovered was that a number of big people's organisations had passionately tackled the issue of burnout before it reached a crisis point.

For a start, they had asked themselves 'was 24/7 contact really necessary'? Simple corporate, cultural changes such as no e-mails after 7pm or before 7am seemed to make a difference allowing leaders to completely switch off and recover without feeling guilty. Flexible, annual, work patterns based on operational or seasonal demands, lateral development to combat repetitive work, routine mentor meetings, shorter summer hours and study leave were just some other concepts currently being considered to safeguard their diminishing talent pool from burning out.

Promoting healthy eating and exercise had also been highly effective. Some Big People's organisations had already seen a difference by discounting gym membership for team members, providing fresh fruit, insisting on regular breaks and stamping out the, 'sandwich at the desk' lunch culture.

While these were positive steps, nothing could replace the need for realism. The most important thing that clever Big People's organisations did was to look at the workload handled by their leaders and ask them themselves honestly, was this expectation realistic?

Lord Seren was encouraged by his findings.

When they returned and shared their findings there was a level of excitement in the air. There were solutions, there were tried and tested ideas tumbling out in the meeting, all with successful outcomes. Lord Seren was probably the most excited of them all. "Just imagine if we could improve the health of the whole Domain. Why not? Single communities have done it so why not a whole Domain? Just imagine if we reduced the sickness right across the Domain by concentrating on folks' well-being. Wouldn't that be amazing? If we could spot leaders who were starting down the burnout escalator and help develop them to cope. Wouldn't that be marvellous? And best of all, if we could help some of the burnt out leaders recover back up to their original positions, wouldn't that be a startling achievement?"

Flootnote: 'Develop your people so they can leave, treat them well so they don't want to'

Flootnote: Never compare yourself with the worst; only ever compare yourself with the best

Chapter Eight

THE DIFFICULT CONVERSATION

ord Seren decided his presence at the 'difficult conversation' might inhibit the discussion, so absented himself from the meeting.

A 'Tea and Crumpets Meeting' was hurriedly convened by the trio to address the problem. Now a 'Tea and Crumpets Meeting' may sound like a gentle afternoon tea party, but it is a very serious leadership meeting indeed and has quite specific rules:

1. Only one problem may be discussed at a 'Tea and Crumpets' meeting ensuring total focus by everyone.
2. Everyone must come to the meeting prepared.

3. The meeting table must be fairly groaning with tea, crumpets, jam, cream, blueberries, strawberries, silver cutlery and Rose Cottage crockery.
4. Nobody can leave the meeting until the one problem has been solved to everyone's satisfaction and all the crumpets have been eaten and all the tea drunk.

The three Senior Leaders of Ten-Tree-Wood sat in silence waiting for Floot, each apprehensive in their own way.

Twenty minutes late, Floot rushed into the meeting dropping papers all over the floor from the files he was carrying. He briefly apologised for his tardiness, hinting he may have to leave early, as he needed to be somewhere else.

The three listened in silence as Floot filled his plate with crumpets, jam and cream which he ate at 100 mph, dominating the conversation with day-to-day problems. With his mouth full of crumpets, jam and cream he fired questions at them in turn.

"Dandelion, will you be able to read this report for the Domain Queen before I send it this afternoon?"

"Dai-Full-Pelt, did you know there was congestion in Market Street again on market day? Can we talk about it when, whatever this meeting is about, has finished?"

"Barley, I need the financial figures for the new, Old Folks' Hom…"

"Please stop," said Dai-Full-Pelt courteously but with authority. "This meeting hasn't been convened for you to discuss everyday problems with us. It's a 'Tea and Crumpets Meeting' and, as the originator of Tea and Crumpets Meetings, you know very well it has only one item on the agenda. That item is you!"

There was silence while Floot tried to understand what in the world could be more important than getting the report to the Domain Queen, sorting out the congestion in Market Street or the really important figures for the new, Old Folks' Home. Then it dawned on him as jam trickled down his chin.

"Me? What about me?"

Barley continued: "Floot, you're here but you're not here. Your mind is somewhere else all the time. We're all worried to death about you. We all believe you are burning out. You can't keep going like this."

"Phoo, hoo. I'm fine, really fine you don't need to worry about me", he said, with a dismissive wave of his hand. "That's very kind of you all, but let me assure you I'm full of beans. I'll let you know if I'm not."

Reaching down into his bag of papers, Floot proceeded to spread them out on the table before he continued: "Now, there really are a few things about the community I'd like to discuss with you, so, if you are all happy I'm OK and I'm not going to fall over at any time, could we run quickly through them please?"

The worried looks around the table told him that everything was not fine and the matter was far from over. There was a long pause as more tea was poured by Dandelion.

"How are you sleeping?" asked Dandelion.

"Look, I'm telling you all I'm fine. I don't want time off and I certainly don't want to talk to anyone from Occ-Health, neither do I want a holiday, start flower pressing or grow my own vegetables."

Floot's volume was rising slightly and the three of them could hear an edge coming on his voice. History had taught them that this edge on his voice often preceded an outburst which, when caught on an off day, this normally mild mannered leader could take the skin off the recipient's back with his tongue. But today Floot's eyes were slightly wet, which told them the conversation could go one of two other ways. Either, Floot could feel threatened, erect barriers, get very angry, protect his seniority by not talking, collect his things and leave the meeting, or on the other hand he might crumble. All three felt uncomfortable.

Floot sat down again slowly, gathered himself, and said: "Look I'm very well and there's nothing wrong with me. There are nights when I don't sleep as well as I should but everyone has nights like that don't they?"

"How's your bad back?" asked Dandelion.

"Now you mention it, it's giving me gyp. I must remember to drop in to see Old Snoz for some more painkillers. I'm sure it'll go soon but it gets worse as the day goes on."

"When was your last square meal?"

Floot brightened for here was something he could be positive about: "Well, only last night one of the fairies dropped off a huge casserole for me. It was delicious."

"A meal you cooked yourself?"

"Oh, I haven't got time to be faffing about cooking. There's far too much to do. I get a pie and chips and apple crumble for pudding from the corner shop at lunchtime. It's lovely and sees me through."

"When was the last time you had a social night out?"

"Oh, recently I think, the other week or was it last month. Oh, I can't remember, anyway why does it matter?"

"Still enjoy work?"

"Yes, love it, I really do, all the cut and thrust of everyday woodland business. The banter and the challenges from on high in the Domain, the ups and the downs..." There was a very long pause and Floot's voice noticeably lowered. "And the downs... and the downs... and the downs." His mood also visibly changed from his current artificial, everything is OK façade to a more sombre tone.

"To be honest, right now I'm struggling a bit. There seem to be far more downs than ups, in fact I'm hard-pressed to think of any ups at all. I'm sure my mood reflects on you guys. I know I've become grumpy and cynical with other folk, I'm becoming more and more disinterested in the job and I lack any form of satisfaction. When I do achieve any of our targets I'm that busy: I'm on the next target, and the next target, and the next. I never have any time to celebrate like we used to. I'm trying to be everything to everyone and I feel if I stop, everything in Ten-Tree-Wood will."

Floot shook his head slowly from side to side. "You've no idea of the pressures. They're relentless and the stresses are ridiculous. She's reduced our budgets again and She's plucking nonsensical target times out of the air and you'll never believe what She's asked for now."

Floot put his head in his hands and sighed to himself. He just sat there rocking for a moment. There was stillness from the anxious trio as they watched their friend trying to come to terms with the problem. Then he started. Floot talked to nobody in particular and to himself for the first time articulating exactly how he felt. They let him talk and talk and talk. Nearly an hour went past before he stopped.

"You can't keep it up," said Barley quietly.

"I know, but so often I've thought, if I can just get to the weekend or the next financial quarter, life will be better or, I just need one good night's sleep. But I find myself wishing for the next weekend after that and the next financial quarter after that and… and… parsnip wine doesn't work anymore!"

"How can we help?"

"Just listening to me let off steam helps. I'm better now. Thanks for letting me rant for a while. You are a good team." And, with that, Floot rose to straighten his papers and leave, but before he could make a move towards the door Barley said: "Just a minute Floot, it was you who taught us never, ever, to leave a 'Tea and Crumpets Meeting' without a written down plan or the whole meeting will have been a complete waste of time and nothing will change. So what's the plan?"

Floot sat down again. Barley poured some fresh tea; Dandelion buttered a crumpet for him and another for herself.

Dai-Full-Pelt began: "Let's start by looking at the Central Domain's new work culture. We know the work culture has changed with the appointment of the new Domain Queen, so how would you describe it now?"

Floot didn't hesitate: "Targets, targets, targets. No compassion, no leeway, no prisoners and definitely no failures."

"OK, have you asked yourself by what the new Domain Queen is being measured?"

"Who cares?"

"It's really important."

"Well, she did tell a meeting of all the Community Leaders she was primarily being measured on the financial growth of the Central Domain and that every community had to contribute significantly. She concluded with the 'not so veiled threat' that there was little margin for error!" remembered Floot.

"Culture change can be good or bad," Dai-Full-Pelt suggested, "but for us to function as a community we must first understand the drivers of the new Domain culture. Confusion only arises when the drivers are vague or inconsistent. To be fair to the new Domain Queen, culture drivers are rarely as clearly defined as She has set them out. For us, that's really good news."

"It is? It doesn't seem like good news from where I'm standing."

"It really is. Without knowing the drivers, leaders burn themselves out putting all their effort into the wrong things. Think about it."

"So what you are saying," said Floot thoughtfully, "is that every decision made in Ten-Tree-Wood should be aligned with Her financial drivers of the new Domain culture?"

"Yes and the three of us must be mindful of Her drivers as well when we come to you Floot, with community problems. We need to have considered the most appropriate solution from a financial perspective too, for the Domain Queen will be seeing every suggestion you propose to Her wearing myopic, financial, bottom line glasses. Everything else will be totally irrelevant. She will filter out and dump everything else until She's met her targets."

"And I've been sending Her stuff that impacts on Ten-Tree-Wood's social agenda, road-building schedule and the new plans for the Old Folks' Home. No wonder She seems hacked off with me all the time," mused Floot thoughtfully. "I've never even had a reply from Her.

"Culture change is OK. It doesn't create burnout on its own. What creates burnout is not knowing the new rules, the new drivers or the things by which, the leader of the new culture is being measured."

Dai-Full-Pelt suggested a way forward: "We want to support you. Would you like Barley to look at all the financials with you and take

67

out all of those projects that don't fit with the drivers of the new culture?"

Floot nodded his acceptance.

"If we know the drivers of the new culture then the next step is to understand the catalysts that create burnout. Tell us what's giving you so much grief and keeping you awake at night?"

"Too many jobs, huge volume of work, unrealistic targets, lack of resources and a skills gap. The Domain Queen has no recognition of the size of some of the jobs She allocates to me or the time required to undertake them. She has no understanding of the consequences of some of Her demands. I just have too many plates spinning at any one time. If I'm really honest, I'm exhausted," said Floot with an uncharacteristic note of surrender in his voice.

"Just exactly how many plates are you spinning at any one time?"

"Millions," snapped Floot.

"Have you ever recorded the number of activities you've been asked to work on?"

"No."

"Perhaps you should."

"If I did, it would definitely show Her just how busy I am and would be tangible evidence that what I am being asked to do is impossible."

There was a delay while he considered the merits of trying to put all of his thoughts onto a plan.

"I suppose I could also show on the plan when things are due to be sent to Her rather than trying to keep it all in my head. That would help me prioritise. That would be a good result from this meeting wouldn't it? Then, when She asked me for more stuff or gave me a new project, I could show Her my plan and then She could make the decision which of Her projects could be rescheduled rather than me just accepting more and more work."

The fog was clearing for Floot. He could see a solution and a helpful logic coming from the meeting.

"May I help you draw up the plan of all the plates you're spinning? We could highlight the catalysts that are causing you stress and categorise them as what you want to do against what you have to do?" asked Dai-Full-Pelt.

"I'd like that. It would make things so much clearer for me. A problem shared and all that…"

"Now we know the drivers of the new culture and the catalysts that are causing you to burn out perhaps we can suggest someone to help you stay on track. Would you consider Lord Seren as your Recovery Buddy? He's been watching you burning out, is as worried as we are and offered to help if you would like."

"Hmmm. Lord Seren. I'd not considered him as someone to help me think. I'd see working with him as facilitated thinking time. Great, the answer is definitely yes. I like Lord Seren, he talks a lot of sense and knows his way around the politics of the Domain and will stop me blundering around making a complete fool of myself sending Her plans of Ten-Tree-Wood's new, Old Folks' Home."

The tension was all around the table when Dandelion, with a twinkle in her eye, broke the atmosphere: "And if we all help and get our old Floot back, perhaps we can get your bell ringing again."

A beetroot-red-faced embarrassed Floot said: "I didn't know anyone else knew about that!"

They all laughed.

***

With the culture defined, the catalysts that were causing Floot's burnout identified and a 'Recovery Buddy' chosen, the four of them left the 'Tea and Crumpets Meeting' with a plan.

Flootnote: Remember, you only have seventy summers. If you are fifty-six years old decide how you will spend your remaining fourteen summers…

Chapter Nine

FINALLY...

Floot did return to his place at the top of the escalator. It took about three months and now he is leading the community as he had so successfully led them previously.

Barley took the finances of the community apart alongside Floot and then put them back together again, but this time they were focussed on the new Domain Queen's agenda (with a little put to one side for secret community projects).

Dai-Full-Pelt and Floot put onto a plan all the 'plates' Floot thought he was spinning on his own and surprisingly there weren't as many as he thought. Just writing them down gave clarity to the jumble of worries tumbling around in his head and, to be fair, it was a huge task, but not impossible. Together they identified each project start and finish dates and allocated the resources required.

Floot met his 'Recovery Buddy' Lord Seren, who adopted a mix of 'Positive Psychology' to re-energise Floot's vitality and 'Strength-Based Coaching Techniques'. Using these techniques, Lord Seren concentrated on Floot's strengths to maximise his effectiveness and rebuild his self-esteem rather than trying to rectify his weaknesses. Lord Seren also managed to bring to the surface some of Floot's other under-utilised strengths currently buried by daily firefighting and minutiae. At each meeting, mindfulness and staying focused on Floot's vision of the future were top of the agenda. These techniques quickly helped Floot regain control of his life.

For his part Floot stopped depending on parsnip wine, started eating healthily and getting exercise again. The colour started to come back into his grey face, the weight started to drop off him and his old vivacity started to reappear.

Two passionate, 'white knights' were chosen from the long list of volunteers to head up the Ten-Tree-Wood Health and Well-Being Strategy. Their objective was to address the poor health of some of the other talented leaders and help generally combat corporate burnout. This was not to be a separate project but part of the 'SPIRIT' of Ten-Tree-Wood. Floot led the way by being at every event they organised. They started with weight management programmes supported by personal trainers, followed by breakfast wellness clinics. Close behind came sleep clinics and stress audits and as their enthusiasm became infectious in the community, more and more ordinary folk joined in wanting to be part of this new Ten-Tree-Wood wellness.

A long-term strategy embedding a coaching and mentoring culture into Ten-Tree-Wood was agreed by the Senior Leadership Team as a talent acceleration strategy and for the early identification of those leaders at risk from corporate burnout.

And Floot's bell did ring again…

And they all lived happily ever after.

Flootnote:
Never waste a
good crisis!

Chapter Ten

THE SERIOUS BIT

REAL LIFE SUCCESS STORIES OF HOW SOME AMAZING LEADERS BURNT OUT AND RECOVERED TO EXCEED THEIR ORIGINAL CORPORATE POSITIONS.

Whilst the Ten-Tree-Wood story confirms that some leaders who burn out are unable to resume their original seniority or position, of those who were able to resume their original seniority within the research population, the author was able to identify common recovery strategies, shared here to assist organisational leaders who recognise they, or members of their team, are burning out.

1.
Position: Territory Manager.
Age at start of burnout: 29. **Gender:** F
Burnout triggers: Excessive hours, unreasonable targets, isolated by working from home for the first time, not enjoying work, out of comfort zone and drowning, juggling busy family and work.
Duration of burning out: Six months.
Off work sick: Six weeks with anxiety.
Personal issues: Death of a cherished relative, continually took on responsibility for others.
Physical changes: Lost some weight, body rejected anti-depressants.
Recovery strategy: Counselling, happy place tape, meditation.
Return: Only temporarily.
Recovery Buddy: None, but I wish I had.
Current Position: Now Director, now understand myself, learned how to control anxiety, now happy.

2.
Position: Director.
Age at start of burnout: 45. **Gender:** F
Burnout triggers: Self-imposed targets, 'where perfect is the enemy of good'.
Duration of burning out: Four years
Off work sick: Infrequently only as a result of reduced immune system and headaches.
Personal issues: Bereavement.

Physical changes: Some sleep deprivation, weight gain and loss, no spark, tearful, overwhelmed anxiety attacks

Recovery strategy: Volunteering, running with a running buddy, focussed on own health and wellbeing over an extended period of time. Read widely about diet, health and mindfulness.

Return: Complete

Recovery Buddy: Peer colleagues, counsellor and hypnosis to consolidate recovery.

Current position: Back at work and firing on all cylinders, life in order, comfortably performing at an enhanced capacity, capable of much more.

3.

Position: Manager.

Age at start of burnout: 35. **Gender**: F.

Burnout triggers: Pressure and volume of work, self-imposed targets.

Duration of burnout: Three years.

Off work sick: Physically couldn't move, complete breakdown.

Personal issues: Persistent clashes with relative.

Physical changes: Lost weight, lost shine on hair.

Recovery strategy: No contact with relative, sees pressure differently, repositioned life, time for w/e hobbies.

Return: Complete.

Recovery Buddy: Peer colleague and counselling for courage.

Current position: Back, taking business to new heights.

4.

Position: Director.

Age at start of burnout: 36. **Gender:** M

Burnout triggers: Fear of failure, change of job, the 'what if monster'. Poor boss, poor culture, poor workforce; any one is hard, all three, impossible.

Duration of burnout: Four years.

Off work sick: None, until appendectomy, off two weeks then off permanently.

Personal issues: Became detached from family, little time at home.

Physical changes: Coffee intake eight cups a day, adrenal fatigue.

Recovery strategy: Walking and talking with wife, diet change, therapy, meditation, counsellor, reviewing what is really important.

Return: Never went back!

Recovery Buddy: Wife, a professional therapist and a mental health relative.

Current position: Independent, happy, ready to take on new challenges, learned many lessons never to be repeated, capable of exceeding all previous levels of responsibility. Now running two new businesses and flourishing with a new love of life. Retired from stress!

5.

Position: Business Development Manager USA.

Age at start of burnout: 50. Gender: F.

Burnout triggers: Overload commuting to USA, only senior woman in business, took on too much, self-imposed targets, living two lifestyles, isolation, didn't have time to care.

Duration of burning out: Two+ years.

Off work sick: No.

Personal issues: Parents both ill. Renovating home.

Physical changes: Sleep deprivation. Irregular hours, tired through time zones, no increase in coffee or alcohol.

Recovery strategy: One month off sick, time to think, walked away. Went into simple charity work while clearing head, ended up transforming finances of the charity, saved £30,000. As a result, quickly regained positivity and self-esteem.

Return: Never went back, except to tidy up.

Recovery Buddy: No, but I wish I had.

Current position: Business Development Executive, loving life, 'best place I've ever been', self-actualisation complete. 'Now I'm kind to myself'.

6.

Position: Regional Manager.

Age at start of burnout: 32. **Gender:** M.

Burnout triggers: Working away from home three days a week. High mileage, anxious all the time, small jobs became big jobs in my eyes, no relationship with my boss, didn't think he ever believed in me, little direction.

Duration of burning out: Two years.

Off work sick: No.

Personal issues: Young family, but who hasn't.

Physical changes: Put on weight, increased rate of smoking, sleep challenges, coffee intake rocketed but alcohol stayed roughly the same.

Recovery strategy: Off work completely for two months, gradually increased exercise, gradually lost weight, gradually felt better about myself, and stopped smoking.

Return: Phased.

Recovery buddy: Loads of friends told me I couldn't keep going at this rate but had no solution except tell me to leave. One trained person to confide in regularly would have helped.

Current Position: Eventually left, then boss was sacked. I was invited back in his role, sales increased three-fold across the UK. Now I look forward to going to work each day.

Chapter Eleven

RELECTIONS FOR ORGANISATIONS

The above are a sample of real life stories of high-performing leaders, who burnt out completely but recovered to exceed their original levels of seniority. Some recovery strategy commonalities from the total research group are documented below, incorporating considerations for organisations:

1. In all cases of high-performing leaders who burnt out, their line leaders neglected to support them as they started their decline. The line leaders either trivialised or dismissed suggestions that the workload was too great. Some line leaders were not sufficiently experienced to have a solution themselves and hence, ignored the problem or in the absence of a solution, threatened 'capability'.

    Organisations should consider developing all levels of leaders to recognise the early signs of burnout.

2. The importance of a 'Recovery Buddy' cannot be over-stated. It was recognised by many in the total research group that an independent, Recovery Buddy would have prevented those, who were at least two-thirds of the way down the escalator, from crashing and burning. However, when they did crash and burn at the bottom of the escalator then a skilful Recovery Buddy would have been a Godsend.

    Organisations should identify suitable internal or external 'Recovery Buddies' and encourage early intervention. A supporting network of Recovery Buddies to discuss alternative approaches and trends in different parts of the organisation is essential.

3. Burning out leaders who regularly replaced critical recovery periods i.e. evenings and week/ends with work, did not realise it at the time but, had started on the road to ruin. Remember the animal example? Animals that regularly came under stress created stress-free periods in which to recover. Without critical recovery periods their chances of survival were significantly reduced. Many of the research respondents

admitted they had slowly eroded their critical recovery periods and confessed that they took nowhere near their holiday allowance. Working extra hours was their short-term answer to long-term problems. In hindsight, the outcome of significantly and regularly depleted recovery periods was obvious.

Organisations should consider adopting the following mantra for all levels of leadership.

'Work hard. Recover hard. Repeat.'

4. Mirror reflections of their physical selves demonstrated, to many of these burnt out leaders, just how far from their previous body shape, overall condition and wellbeing they had fallen. In many cases sports had been abandoned, gym membership lapsed, swimwear no longer fitted and the bicycle had become as rusty as an old horseshoe! The mirror acted as an embarrassing wake-up call. How could they expect to recover and become fit to lead their organisations if the engine for thought and action had been so neglected? What image did it display? A significant number of respondents addressed their personal wellbeing as a matter of priority. Diet, health and exercise became a way of life for many and continued long past their return to work.

   Organisations should upgrade their 'well-being' strategies in the light of the research into the decline of employee health.

5. Some leaders who crashed and burned eventually learned to become comfortable with the chaos of organisational change for the first time in their working lives. Volume had in the main dragged them down, not the challenge or complexity of any one part. They began to understand that their desire for order and symmetry at work did not reflect the reality of corporate life and, as such, they were unlikely ever to be comfortable. Examining the boundaries of chaos with a Recovery Buddy helped them rebalance their priorities.

Developing Recovery Buddies in 'Strengths-Based Coaching Techniques' should be a priority for organisations.

6. Learning how to have the difficult conversation with team members who were underperforming, learning to constructively say no to senior leaders without fear, understanding the impact of the Quality/Acceptance Nexus and the criticality of effective delegation helped some regain control of their lives and self-esteem.

    Enhancing interpersonal skills and embedding the concept of the Quality/Acceptance Nexus across organisations reduces confusion, drives quality and reduces the need for re- work.

Flootnote: Whilst these are the top six recovery strategies adopted by high performing leaders and reflections for organisations, nothing can replace the necessity for realism of expectation, by all levels of leader, to prevent the destruction of high-performing talent in the first place